MW00529544

Fun & Games with GRANDMA

Traveling with your grandkids, eating out, enjoying nature, and simply sharing quiet times are a grandma's delight … especially if you have this collection of engaging activities! In Fun & Games with Grandma, you'll find hours of enjoyment for kids of all ages. Card games – with punch-out cards ready to play – boredom busters, word puzzles and art activities, outdoor experiences, and travel tips will keep you and your grandkids entertained in almost any situation. You'll have all the kids saying, "Grandma, you're the best!" Now, who doesn't want to hear that?

These projects are recommended for children 8 and above. Grandparents, always carefully supervise your grandchildren when enjoying these activities together, especially around water, in the kitchen, or when using sharp objects. Remember that any activity involving small parts can present a choking hazard and is not suitable for children under the age of 3. Before beginning any activity, take into consideration your grandchildren's ages, abilities, and any allergies they may have, and adapt your plans accordingly. Stay safe and have fun!

Fun & Games With Grandma
ISBN 978-1-7336250-9-8
Published by Product Concept Mfg., Inc., 2175 N. Academy Circle #201, Colorado Springs, CO 80909
©2019 Product Concept Mfg., Inc. All rights reserved.
Written and Compiled by Andrea W. Doray in association with Product Concept Mfg., Inc.

Don't you love being a grandma?

Inside *Fun & Games with Grandma*, you'll find games, activities, and events to enjoy with your grandkids. Check out "Grandma's Grab Bag" for no-prep ideas and play staples to always have on hand. "Boredom Busters" are just that … you can even have fun waiting in line! With ordinary items such as masking tape, construction paper, child-safe markers, you can make extraordinary things. You'll also discover arts and crafts, outdoor adventures, and memory- and vocabulary-building activities. Plus, check out our very own punch-and-play card games!

Of course, we know how important quiet time is with your grandchildren, so we've included ideas to share those special moments, too.

Start your adventure in *Fun & Games with Grandma* … and take your grandkids with you!

Sweet, Fun, and Memorable Ways to Engage with Your Grandchildren

- Walk hand-in-hand with your grandchildren, with no particular place to go.
- Ask them to tell you about a special memory.
- Take time to smell the roses, literally: ask the kids to smell flowers, indoors or out.
- Ask kids questions that don't require a simple yes or no answer.
- Listen carefully to what your grandkids tell you, without judgement or advice.
- Enjoy a family group hug, even if you are with only grandchildren!
- Look up at the stars on a clear evening.
- Observe the moon … what do you see?
- Sing a favorite song together.
- Hold hands and walk or dance around in a circle, maybe singing that favorite song!
- Take turns making funny faces at each other.

- Practice somersaults, crab walks, and walking on their hands.
- Try something new together – walk to a new park, try a new food, listen to new music. The possibilities are endless!
- Lay in the grass and watch the clouds drift and change above you.
- Make snow angels.
- Watch water drip from trees, flowers, or your house after it rains.
- Walk through the yard and have the kids touch the different textures around them.
- Ask the kids to teach you something!
- Read together, of course … snuggle in a big chair!
- Listen to the different songs of birds.
- Watch the wind rustle through the trees.
- Watch the sunset … and the sunrise!

Share amazement at the wonders of God's creation!

Grandma's Grab Bag

When you need games to play with your grandkids –
now – look no further than this collection of activities that
require little-to-no prep or props. Keep these ideas handy
for fast fun whenever you want it!

INSIDE OUT

Get the giggles going when you ask grandkids to wear their
clothes inside out. If you're enjoying fun time with more than one
grandchild, ask the kids to swap their coats or sweaters and wear
someone else's clothes inside out.

INSIDE/OUTSIDE

It doesn't matter what the weather is! Play this game by asking
kids what things inside the house could be used outdoors, including
obvious items such as umbrellas, hats, jackets, snow boots.
- Help kids plan activities they might have outside, such as a
  picnic with tablecloth, napkins, plates, and spoons.
- What about an outdoor concert with the kids' musical
  instruments and card table chairs for the audience?
  (A piano might not work for this one!)
- Consider blankets and pillows that can be used for
  "camping" in the back yard. Throw in a toothbrush for
  good measure.
- BONUS: If the weather is good, take any or all of these
  items outside and have fun!

GRANDMA SAYS ...

Yes, kids can enjoy it when Grandmas tells them what to do! This game works especially well with a group of grandkids (and their friends, too) but it's just as much fun with two of you.

- Give kids instructions such as, "Grandma says close your eyes and stick out your tongue," or "Grandma says sit down and touch your nose to your knees."
- Add in some silly and tricky directions such as, "Grandma says pat your head. Grandma says rub your tummy at the same time!"
- Ask kids to repeat fun tongue twisters, including these old-timers ... or any favorites of your own: "rubber baby buggy bumpers" and "she sells sea shells by the seashore."
- P.S. If the kids need to do some chores or get ready for bed, try mixing up the instructions, such as, "Grandma says brush your hands and wash your teeth."

TWENTY QUESTIONS

Kids never seem to tire of this "Guess What" game. Choose an object you see (in the room, outdoors, etc.,) and allow kids to ask you 20 "yes/no" questions to guess what it is. TIP: You know your grandkids best ... they can ask questions other than yes/no if you prefer.

- Choose a person they know – family members, school buddies, church friends – and ask kids to guess who it is using the 20-question format.

Grab Bag Of Things To Keep On Hand

- Books - Pictures, puzzles, riddles, & more

- Big balls of yarn

- Puzzles

- An assortment of yo-yos

- Plastic interlocking building blocks

- Pipe cleaners in lots of colors and lengths

- String for simple games, such as Jacob's Ladder with your hands

- Mini cars … make tunnels from empty cardboard paper towel tubes!

- Blow-up balls (they come with a pump!) that have a plastic ring on top just right for bouncing.

- Plastic-wand-in-the-bottle types of bubbles. Get several bottles in different colors!

- If the weather's nice and you have room in the yard (parks are great, too!), try out a long swisher wand or the big round hoop type of bubble wand.

- Have the wand but not the bubbles? Have kids measure and mix 1/2 cup water with 1/4 cup liquid dish detergent and 1 tsp. sugar. Kids can use right away or leave the mixture overnight for a longer lasting solution.

Boredom Busters

Have you ever been faced with the "but-Grandma-there's-nothing-to-do!" syndrome? Of course you have! Bust your grandkids' boredom with these creative and interesting activities, no matter where you are.

WHISPERS IN THE DARK

With a bandana, scarf, or anything that's handy, make a comfortable blindfold for the kids. Using whispers, help them navigate around the room or the house. For added curiosity, direct them to the sink and then whisper instructions for turning on the water to wash their hands or brush their teeth. It's also fun – but a bit messy – to guide them through eating soup or pasta!

MAKE BEAUTIFUL MUSIC TOGETHER

It's always fun to share your talent with grandkids if you play a musical instrument, but you can also make beautiful music together just by filling up glasses with various levels of water. Ask kids to tap the sides of the glasses with a fork to produce the different tones. Make up your own songs and share them with others!

CARDS, ANYONE?

Regular playing cards yield a variety of interesting games you can play almost anywhere! Grab a deck and ask kids to:
- stack cards of each color.
- stack cards of each suit/shape.
- stack cards from ace to king, using any combinations of suits.
- stack cards from ace to king one suit at a time.
- stack all the aces, twos, threes, etc., together.
- stack cards backwards, in each suit or a combination of them all.

ALPHABET STICKIES

Armed with a sticky note pad, write one letter of the alphabet on a sheet and ask the kids to stick the note onto something in the room that starts with that letter. Continue through the alphabet as kids place their notes. Write multiple stickies with the same letter when kids identify more items and see how much of the room gets covered!

HIDE-AND-SEEK STICKIES

Grab your trusty sticky note pad and hide a few pages here and there around the house. Use the "hot/cold" method to guide kids as they search for the stickies, or give them directions such as, "Take 10 steps forward and turn to your right. Then walk backwards for 4 steps." Have some fun with your instructions!

What was it like when ...?

Photo albums – especially in this digital era! – are fascinating journeys through time for the grandkids.

1. Choose a family member, such as a mother or father (or yourself), and walk the kids through their life.
2. Point out the differences in clothes and hair and cars and furniture.
3. Take pictures of the kids and place them next to your photo or their parents' photos when you were the same age. You may have to go to a drugstore or big box retailer to get prints made unless you have an instamatic camera.
4. Talk about the changes that have occurred since their family members were their own ages!

Snowflake or Star Shapes

Kids love to create familiar shapes such as snowflakes or stars. On heavy paper or cardboard, have kids layer painter's tape in asterisks to make snowflakes. Kids can dab light blue paint with a sponge around the taped asterisks. When the paint is dry, help kids remove the tape to reveal a beautiful snowflake landscape!

For stars, dark blue is perfect for the background. Kids use five equal lengths of tape to form a star, and then paint or sponge the blue around the stars, careful not to paint inside the outline. Help kids carefully remove the tape when the paint is dry for a night sky scene ... right inside the house!

Say What?

Give kids earplugs or earphones to wear. Have kids take turns talking out loud (without earplugs) as those wearing earplugs try to guess what they are saying. Kids can point at something, act it out, or have the others lip read! Use simple rolled-up tissue as earplugs to play this game anywhere, even when waiting in line, at the doctor's office, or in a restaurant.

Sticky Note Scripture Challenge

Here's a fun game to help grandkids remember Bible scriptures. Write each word of a scripture on a sticky note. Scramble them up on a table and see if your grandkid can put it back in the correct order. This is a great way of helping kids understand the scriptures and the meanings. For an extra challenge, remove one word from the scripture and see if they can find the missing word.

Coupon Gift Books

Kids like to give as much as they like to receive! Help kids prepare coupon books with loving offerings for Father's or Mother's Day, birthdays, or Christmas. Brainstorm ideas with grandkids, such as "Help Dad wash the car," or "Clear off the table after supper." Kids write and draw their coupons on note-sized paper, and Grandma helps staple them together. Have kids design a cover for their coupon books and wrap as gifts!

What's the Plan?

From the comfort of Grandma's living room, plan an outing, imaginary or actual, and ask kids what they would need to take along. Include necessities such as a toothbrush, but stretch their imaginations – and their organizational skills! – by talking about the clothes they'll need for the weather, or what languages they might need to learn. For extra play, have the kids draw or write about their planned adventures.

What Animal Am I?

This perennial favorite is exciting for younger kids as they imitate animals with sounds and movements for you to guess what they are. Add extra interest by discussing where the animals live ... tigers in the jungle, elephants in Asia and Africa, giraffes in Africa, etc. Be sure to take your turn, too!

Where Do They Come From?

Everyone loves maps, so pull out an atlas or spread out some individual maps. Have kids toss a game piece or candy onto a map page and then ask them questions about the locale where they landed. Here are some to get you started:

- What (country, city, state, ocean) did you land on?
- How would you get there (car, airplane, boat, etc.)?
- What language(s) do people speak there?
- What kinds of clothes do the people wear?
- What do their homes look like?
- What games do they play?

Chile: Corre la Guaraca

The name translates to "Run, Run, la Guaraca." Although Chilean kids typically speak Spanish, Guaraca is a nonsense word! Five or more players sit in a circle while a runner jogs around the outer rim with a handkerchief. The seated kids are not allowed to watch. Trying not to be felt, the runner drops the handkerchief on a player's back and continues running. If the runner makes it all the way around the circle before the player realizes they've been touched, the seated player is out. If the seated player does notice, they can jump up and tag the runner, who is then out. Kids take turns as the runner.

Ireland: Catch my Shadow!

One player who is "it" runs around the other players, trying to stand on their shadows to "catch" them. When a player is caught, they become the chaser. Players being chased can also run to a shaded place where they have no shadow and are safe!

Brazil: Luta De Galo

This is a two-player game but more children can play by taking turns. Each player has a handkerchief tucked into a pocket or waistband. Players are not allowed to use their right arms, which are crossed over their chests. Then, hopping on one leg, players must try to capture and win the handkerchief from their opponent using just their left hand!

United Kingdom: Pass the Parcel

Before the game begins, Grandma makes the parcel by wrapping something fun or silly in layer upon layer of paper and tape, with a different pattern or color for each layer. Ask kids to sit in a circle, then turn on some music. Players pass the parcel around until Grandma stops the music. The player holding the parcel when the music stops gets to remove one layer of paper. Grandma starts and stops the music until the final layer of paper is removed. The last player to unwrap the parcel "wins" what's inside!

Lazer Tunnel

What can't you do with painter's tape and crepe paper? Tape different lengths of red crepe paper streamers (for the laser effect!) across a hallway to make the tunnel. Zig zag the paper streamers back and forth and vary the heights from high to low. Kids have to crawl through, step over, and otherwise contort themselves to make their way past the laser beams without touching them!

Zipper Thermometer: What's the temperature?

Attach a large zipper to sturdy construction paper or poster board and use a marker to write temperatures on the board along the sides of the zipper in increments of 10 degrees, such as 40 degrees, 50 degrees, and so forth. Don't forget 0 degrees and negative temperatures, too! Ask kids to read the thermometer (Grandma can help) and zip their zippers to the correct temperatures. Play this zipper thermometer game over several days, or even on one single day as the temperatures outside change from morning to evening. Keep a chart of the temperatures over time so kids see how the temperatures move from cool to warm and back again.

Name Those Pictures

We all know kids love to play with Grandma's smart phone! Instead of streaming games, engage your grandkids with family photos. TIP: Create an album or collection ahead of time on your phone of family pictures, homes, vacation spots – anything kids will recognize. Have kids identify who is in the photos or where they are … kids are always eager to see photos of themselves! Ask the grandkids if they remember what they were doing and how they were feeling. Take some quiet time to talk about what family means and to lift others up in prayer.

Mixed-Up Word Cups!

Looking for a fun, creative learning tool that's easy to make and keeps grandkids engaged? With a marker, write an assortment of 5 letters on 4 or 5 foam, plastic, or paper cups, so that the letters line up in straight columns or rows across when the cups are stacked. Kids turn and rework the cups to see how many words they can create from the letters you included. Add more cups and letters to create a real challenge.

Toss the Box

Find a square box - or make your own! With some sturdy poster board, a little bit of tape, and a marker, you have everything you need for this roll-play game! Cut the poster board into equal-sized squares, large enough to roll or toss out onto the floor when made into a box. Before you tape the board pieces together to make the square, write activities on each side for the kids to act out when they toss the box. Here are some we like:

- Walk backwards around the room.
- Quack like a duck (or make the sounds of any other animals).
- Jump on one foot 10 times.
- Count to 100 in increments of 5 or 10, such as 10, 20, 30, and so on. Raise the number even higher, such as to 1,000 if the kids are able.
- Write or tell a story about _____. You can leave the topic blank when you write out the square and use sticky notes to change it each time!
- Touch all the things in the room that start with "A" or any alphabet letter of your choice. You can also leave this one blank and use sticky notes to vary the letter.
- Say the alphabet backwards.
- Sing their favorite songs.
- Read to you from their favorite books.

Make several different boxes for longer play, and especially if more than one grandkid is playing.

Chalked Up Family Tree

Kids combine chalk art with three-dimensional elements to create a family tree. TIP: Provide as much information as you can about the members of the children's family. Have kids draw a large brown tree trunk with spreading branches green leaves in any shapes they like – a driveway or patio are good places. To make the "family" tree, help kids write the names of family members on the backs of paper plates and place them on the tree with removable putty in the approximate order of family relationships. Make sure they put themselves on the tree! Take photos to share with all the relatives.

Alternatively,

- Kids draw and color faces on the paper plates.
- Grandma prints out photos of the family and kids paste these images on the paper plates.

P.S. This family tree is also a great indoor activity using markers on poster board, with smaller paper plates for the family. Kids can also use brown and green construction paper for the tree. TIP: Brush some buttermilk on the poster board for a smoother surface before drawing with chalk!

Night Sky Gazing

To spend some "brilliant" time together, lie on the grass and look up at the stars on a beautiful clear evening. Point out the planets, and take this chance to really observe the moon ... what do your grandkids see?

Outdoor Outings

As Grandma takes time to explore the natural world together with your grandkids, share conservation and respect for natural resources with these memory-making activities. Help kids understand "Leave No Trace". Resist the temptation to pick wildflowers, collect pinecones, or gather up stones from our national forests. TIP: Encourage kids to follow these guidelines on public land, but do help them collect their natural treasures from local parks, around the neighborhood, and especially in Grandma's yard!

Here are some great ways for kids to enjoy the outdoors with Grandma.

PLANT MY SOCKS!

Kids will be happily surprised to traipse around the park or the woods with Grandma in just their socks! Make sure the kids wear shoes, then pull on a pair of large old cotton socks over them. Use a safe permanent marker to write their names on their socks. Then head out to your favorite place to walk or hike. As kids walk along the trail, their socks pick up material that's on the ground such as seeds, grasses, leaves, etc. TIP: Before you leave for the hike, prepare a moist soil-mix box for kids to plant their socks in when you all come back! If kids are wearing thin cotton socks, you can "plant" the whole sock in the box and cover with about an inch of soil. If kids wore thick socks, like tube socks, cut off just the sole to plant in the box. Keep the box moist and warm – indoors is usually best – and watch with the grandkids to see what grows!

The Natural World ... In Photos

On a simple walk in the woods, Grandma helps kids engage in the wonder of the natural world ... with an instant camera. Kids can take pictures of anything along the way that captures their interest. TIP: Make sure you have plenty of film or use a smartphone and take to a drugstore to make prints.

- Ask the kids to narrate stories along the hike about the photos they choose, perhaps about fictional characters on the hike with you, or about their own experiences.
- Encourage kids to follow themes for their nature photos, such as rocks, flowers, trees, water, or beautiful views.
- When your photos are printed, have small albums or sheets of paper and glue handy for the kids to arrange their photos any way they choose. Ask your grandkids what they found interesting about their various pictures.
- Ask kids to tell or write stories about the photos they captured, and to draw or color other scenes that could go along with their stories.
- Have kids spend a quiet moment with Grandma to say a prayer of thanks for the wonders of nature.

Wacky and Wonderful Walking Sticks

Even a walk around the neighborhood with Grandma is a treat, especially if kids make their own walking sticks. Help kids find a stick that's just the right size for them and have them decorate with child-safe paint or markers, and natural treasures such feathers, fabric streamers, fallen leaves, or shells. Kids can help you make your own wacky and wonderful walking stick, too!

Vagabond Hike

Pretend you are vagabonds and wrap up some goodies and snacks in a hobo sack with your grandkids to wander the world (sort of). Kids will love helping Grandma fill the kerchief and tie it to a stick to carry on their adventures. Place a bandana on a flat surface and smooth it out. Arrange a bag of vagabond bars (recipe follows), a compass, a map, and other outdoor-worthy items in the middle. Pick up two corners of the bandana diagonal from each other, tie them together, and pull the ends of the knot to tighten it. Position the stick over the first knot, about 6 inches away from the end. Draw up the other diagonal two corners and grab the ends of the first knot with them. Tie the corners tightly to the stick to close the bag. Tie another knot to fasten it securely to the stick for your grandkids' vagabond bags!

Vagabond Bars

Measure out and mix 1/2 cup honey, 1 cup powdered milk, and 1 cup sunflower seed butter together. Form the mixture into small balls and roll in granola cereal. Kids love using their hands to press the mixture into balls! Chill and keep ready for your next hobo hike!

TIP: Sunflower seed butter is nut-free with a consistency nearly identical to peanut butter. Find it in the health aisle in most grocery stores or at health and specialty food stores.

Explorer's Map

Don't forget to bring a notebook and markers on your hike! Kids create their own explorer's map by drawing identifying features along the trail such as lakes or meadows or streams. If you're in a more urban setting, use landmarks such as park benches, playgrounds, or flagpoles as signposts for the maps. Kids transfer their drawings to larger sheets or paper for Grandma to follow with them the next time they go out for that hike!

Explorer's Trail Mix

Every explorer needs some nourishment! Start with 1 package of granola cereal and ask the grandkids what else they want in their trail mix! Suggestions include:

- raisins
- banana, mango, or other fruit chips
- dried apricots, pineapple, cranberries, or blueberries
- coconut
- chocolate chips
- mini marshmallows
- sunflower seeds

Have kids combine their ingredients in a zipper plastic bag.

When-We-Get-Back Crafts

After spending time in nature, kids can share their experiences with these crafts and games.

- **Nature Name Writing:** Using found nature materials from Grandma's yard or around the neighborhood, kids spell their names with rocks, twigs, leaves, flower petals, or seeds.

- **Nature Plaques:** Kids paint or color background scenes on paper plates, and then paste twigs, leaves, stones, flowers, or grass for a three-dimensional plaque. Grandma punches a hole in the top of the plate and threads a ribbon through to hang the plaque for display.

- **Twig Painting:** Perfect for a return from the outdoors! Kids use twigs instead of brushes to paint with thick tempera paint on heavy paper. You'll all be surprised at what kids can create.

- **Leaf Placemats:** Have kids collect colorful newly fallen leaves to arrange between two sheets of clear contact paper. Trim the paper to placemat size. TIP: If the leaves are already dry, kids love to crumble them in their hands for the placemats!

- **Leaf Stamp Art:** Kids apply water-based paint to the veined (back) sides of leaves and press them onto construction paper. Making leaf prints of different sizes, shapes, and colors makes an interesting collage!

- **Leaf Shadow Prints:** Place a piece of dark-colored construction paper on a sunny windowsill and have kids arrange leaves they collected from around the neighborhood or Grandma's yard. After several hours, the sun will fade the paper, leaving silhouettes of their finds!

- **Leaf People:** Kids attach real leaves – big ones such as maple leaves work especially well – to sheets of construction paper with a small amount of glue. Kids draw arms, legs, and heads to create their leaf people.

    - TIP: Don't use dry autumn leaves … they will crumble when you try to paste them to the paper.

    - Ask kids to make a leaf person for everyone in their families, complete with hair color!

    - Encourage kids to talk about their friends and create a scene with leaf people friends.

    - Do your grandkids find other shapes, such as animals, in their leaves? Have them draw what they see.

Great Garden Games

Whether you have your hands in the dirt with your grandkids, or enjoy craft gardens indoors, these activities are sure to entertain.

Kids' Picture Garden: Thoroughly wash the tops of egg cartons or the bottoms of plastic foam grocery store food trays for grandkids to make a paper garden! First, have kids spread a layer of dirt on the trays. (Coloring the tray brown also works, or pasting brown construction paper.) Kids cut pictures of vegetables or flowers from magazines and paste the pictures onto small pieces of poster board. Kids can also draw their own. Thread pipe cleaners through slits at the top and the bottom of the pictures, and push the pipe cleaners in rows into the bottom of the tray for this delightful picture garden. TIP: Be careful not to make holes in the trays if you're using real dirt!

My Outdoor Garden with Grandma: For a real garden you share with your grandkids, designate a small section outside just for them. Sow seeds for fast-growing and reliable plants such as lettuce, carrots, or beans with the kids. Track the progress with them as the seeds sprout and produce vegetables.

My Indoor Garden with Grandma: If you don't have space for a garden, sowing seeds in paper, foam, or plastic cups for smaller plants such as flowers can be just as fun. Set a few of these plant cups on a cookie sheet and watch what grows! TIP: Kids can glue pictures from the actual seed packets to the cups.

"Grandma's Garden" Sign: If you have a community garden plot, a flowerbed in the backyard, or a simple set of herbs on the windowsill, your grandkids will get a kick out of creating a sign especially for you. For larger spaces, kids can paint "Grandma's

Garden" or "Flowers by Grandma" on a wooden shingle or plank. Inside, kids use poster board and markers to make signs that say, "Grandma's Windowsill Garden" or "Grandma's Handy Herbs." Brainstorm ideas with your grandkids or just let them surprise you!

Refrigerator Pickles: At harvest time, your grandkids will love to help you make these refrigerator pickles … especially if they come from Grandma's garden! Grandma prepares 9 cups of thinly sliced cucumbers, 1 sliced onion, and 1 cup of sliced or diced green pepper (optional). Kids can measure and mix together 1 cup of vinegar, 2 cups of sugar, 2 Tbls. salt, and a tsp. of celery seed. Pour over the cucumbers in a glass jar – no water processing needed – to store in the refrigerator and enjoy the next time the grandkids come to visit!

Backyard Games

SPONGE WATER-BOMBS

Reusable and washable water-bombs are a "cool" way to beat the summer heat! Play catch or keep-away, have a water-bomb fight, or just chase each other around with these squishy spongy toys. Cut colorful dish sponges into 4 pieces lengthwise. Stack 2 layers of 4 sponge lengths in multiple colors, and tie fishing line or strong string around the middle of the sponges as tight as possible. Soak the sponges in a tub of water outdoors, squish them, and throw them around for lots of grandkid play. Hang sponge water-bombs in a mesh bag to dry.

WE'RE HAVING A HORSE RACE!

Tape out a "racetrack" outdoors, large enough for the kids to run around in it. Give each grandkid an empty wrapping paper cardboard tube for their horses and line everyone up at the starting line. Use a bell or whistle to let them out of the gates … and they're off! (If you want to play an indoor version, have kids race on their knees or all fours.)

SPRINKLER SHOWER

Screw an old shower head onto a garden hose or attach with plumber's tape. Hang the hose over a tree branch and send the water through!

Backyard Water Ping Pong

Kids are excited to compete when they see Grandma setting up the water ping pong game! Fill 10 large plastic drinking cups about 3/4 full of water and line 5 cups across each end of a picnic table. Give kids different colored ping pong balls to toss from behind one end of the table into the cups of water at the other end. Kids can bounce the balls on the table or throw them directly into the cups. Each player gets a chance to throw 5 ping pong balls at each turn. The winner is the player who lands the most ping pong balls in the cups … or the player who gets splashed the most by opponents on the opposite side of the table! Kids can play water ping pong over and over.

Sprinkler Bottle

Kids love to run through water sprinklers, but this pastime is even more fun when they get to make their own! Start with a sturdy plastic liter soda bottle. Kids can use waterproof paint to design their sprinklers before Grandma punches a number of holes into the top and sides of the bottle. Use waterproof tape such as plumber's tape to attach the bottle to a garden hose, turn on the water, and let the fun begin!

Hopscotch...Grandma's Way!

Draw a traditional hopscotch board with chalk, and try one of these fun variations.

"WE ARE ..."

Get started with this affirmation game by writing the phrase "We are ... at the bottom of the grid. In each box, write positive words such as Kind, Happy, Smart, Strong, etc. Kids throw their markers and when they jump in a box, they complete the statement, such as "We are Kind!"

ADD 'EM UP!

Make math fun by chalking numbers into hopscotch boxes. Kids jump into the box from Grandma's instructions, such "1 + 3"... kids jump to box 4. Use as many boxes in the hopscotch grid as you need for higher numbers. Kids can also do subtraction and multiplication with your instructions, such as "3 x 2," and kids jump to box 6.

BOOKS OF THE BIBLE

Another option for the hopscotch grid is to help kids memorize names of Bible books. Write in the New Testament books: Matthew, Mark, Luke, John, etc.

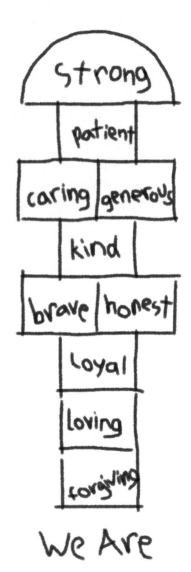

A-maze-ing Star-Gazing

Here's an a-maze-ing way to help kids of all ages reflect on gratitude … plus, whenever they look at the stars, they'll be prompted to think of all they are thankful for! Cut out several star shapes from heavy paper, approximately 5" each. TIP: You can also use 3-inch by 5-inch index cards and add a star sticker to each. In a variation of "wish upon a star," ask the kids: "If you could pray upon a star, what would you give thanks for or what would you like to pray for?" Have kids write their answers on the stars, then construct a star path with blue painter's tape on the floor in a large area. Using a spiral pattern or a back-and-forth zig-zag. You can also tape down lengths of wide colorful ribbon for the maze.

Tape the kids' "prayer request" stars along the maze, about 3 feet apart. Talk with the kids about being quiet and mindful as they proceed through the maze. Have each child follow the maze path, stopping at each star to give thanks or lift up the prayer that's requested. Other children can follow, and kids can experience how soothing it feels when they are still and thoughtful about what they are thankful for. Plus, they all find how nice it feels to know others are praying for them!

Maybe the next time the kids spot a star at night, they'll remember this time spent with you, and stop to "pray upon a star."

Tape-Resist Painting

Have you and the grandkids tried tape-resist art, painting around and over shapes laid out with tape? You'll need that blue painter's tape, large thick paper or poster board, paint brushes and paint (use the washable type if you're painting outside).

Geometrical Shapes

Geometrical tape-type painting is especially engaging because the kids place their own tape on the painting surface, in straight lines up, down, across, diagonally – in any way they want. Then … start painting! Encourage kids to use different colors of paint inside the various spaces between the tape. When the paint is dry, help the kids remove the strips of tape to reveal their extraordinary artwork! TIP: It doesn't matter if paint gets on the tape.

Bean Bag Color Toss

Have kids color chalk circles in a variety of colors, spread out around a concrete area. Prepare ahead by writing each color name several times on different index cards. Mix up the cards so kids pull one card at a time from the deck, and take turns trying to toss their bean bags into a circle that matches that color. Sometimes all the kids get the same color! When everyone has tossed all their bags, the one with the most correct landings is the winner.

Sidewalk Chalk-Talk

You can take your trusty tape outside for chalk art, too! Watch as your grandkids create interactive art and beautiful designs, as well as participate in games you help them draw out, on a smooth surface such as a sidewalk or driveway. TIP: If you want chalk art to last for a week or so, soak the chalk in water before use.

Long Jump with Chalk

To get grandkids really moving, draw horizontal lines in a series on the sidewalk in distances that kids can easily reach by jumping. Give kids different colors of chalk and challenge them to jump as far as they can to land on their feet. Have them record their landings with their chalk colors. Vary the instructions to jump on one foot or even backwards!

Shadow Drawings

Have kids line up their favorite toys, characters, or animals with the bright sun behind them. Kids can draw around the shapes formed by the shadows and use chalk to color in the outlines.

Sidewalk Chalk Name Game

Inside a simple grid of 36 squares, kids jump from space to space to spell their names! Enter alphabet letters randomly around the grid so they aren't in order, and scatter the other 10 spaces as blanks throughout. Kids start out with the first letters of their first names and jump to each of the subsequent letters. The blank boxes are free spaces where kids can land when jumping from letter to letter if the alphabet boxes are too far away.

- For variation, have kids jump from letter to letter in alphabetical order – or reverse order.

Bean Bag Bingo

Use the alphabet grid described in "Sidewalk Chalk Name Game" (above) to play some special sidewalk bingo, as well! Have 4 bean bags for each child in the game. Write the letters of the alphabet with a heavy marker on index cards, add 10 blank cards for the empty boxes, and shuffle the cards. Kids take turns drawing a card from this alphabet deck. TIP: Insert cards randomly back into the deck to keep playing longer. Kids take turns tossing their bean bags at the letters (or blanks) on their cards. When kids have tossed all their bags, the one with the most correct landings is the winner. It's also fun to have kids try to land on the letters of their names.

Chalk Dots

Take this pencil-and-paper game outside to create an interactive version with a chalk grid of dots – the larger the better for multiple players. Kids take turns drawing lines to connect two dots either horizontally or vertically, trying to close the lines to form a box. Kids can write their names in boxes they form, or color in their squares. After the board is complete, count the names or the colors to find the winner.

Interactive Chalk Art

Kids love interactive chalk art, so be sure to take photos as they pose with their creations! Start by brainstorming ideas with the kids about what they want to be or do in their art – an astronaut, a superhero, a pirate? Climb the beanstalk or ride a magic carpet? Kids can blow out birthday candles on a giant chalk cake, ride on swings in a playground, or swim under the ocean. Look at pictures in books and magazines or online with your grandkids for inspiration. It's often useful to sketch out the drawings on large pieces of craft paper to use as guidelines for outlining the art. Kids use lots of colorful chalk to create their scenes, and then position themselves on the surface to become part of their creations. With an instant camera, take multiple photos for the kids to share with family and friends!

Strike the pose!

On a sunny day, grandkids pose themselves in wacky or funny positions to cast crazy shadows. After Grandma or another grandkid chalks an outline around their shadows, kids can color inside silly shadows!

Tape-Resist Chalk Art

What would chalk art be without some tape-resist play? Use tape to outline words, shapes, animals, letters, numbers on the ground. Kids chalk over the taped areas, in an overall color for an outline of the shape the tape is removed, or they can color inside the lines. Peel off the tape carefully to reveal the art!

Nature Rainbows

What is it about rainbows that both grandkids and grandmas love? Make this extra-special rainbow with sidewalk chalk and nature's bounty. Kids chalk out arched layers in rainbow colors and then add leaves, grass, flower petals, stones on top … anything they want to create their designs. Use an instant camera to capture the rainbows.

On-The-Go Games

Traveling with kids is enjoyable … most of the time. To head off the inevitable "Are we there yet?" questions, rely on these activities to entertain your grandkids whether you're on a road trip, traveling by plane, or are simply out for a meal together.

BACKSEAT BINGO

Play bingo with a twist! Prepare these picture and writing boards before a road trip. At the top of a piece of poster board, write words or phrases that describe what kids are likely to see on the trip – a train, cows in a field, purple flowers, a bus. Outline blank squares on the boards for kids to draw any of the things they spot along the way. Ask kids to compose a poem or story for at least one of the items they found.

- Ask kids to make up a story from what they experienced on the journey, using make-believe characters and settings.

- Encourage kids to draw additional scenes to illustrate their stories.

- If your grandkids will be away from home for a while, they can write a letter to their families about what they saw, and add some of the drawings, poems, or stories they created.

Oldies But Goodies

Here are some new updates to old games, just in time for your next trip with the grandkids!

- Have kids design their own license plates.

- Have kids keep track of the license plates they see ... try to get every state!

- Wrap small toys and surprises in paper maps of their destinations. Have kids open them at each stop.

- As a group, locate words on signs and billboards that start with letters of the alphabet, in order. Some letters are harder than others! If kids have trouble spotting more difficult letters such as Q and X, they can look for words that contain those letters, such as "exit."

Fundays of the Week

A game for today, tomorrow, or any day of the week! Ask kids to make up funny names or rhymes, such as:
- Windy Wednesday or Flyday Friday.
- If it's Thirsty Thursday, have a root beer float together.
- Plus, whether it's Stormy Saturday or Sunny Sunday, any of the activities here are entertaining for everyone!

Words That Stick

Kids are really attracted to this game! Give each grandkid a metal cookie sheet and magnetic alphabet letters. Kids can spell their names, make up words, and trade letters with others. Magnets in geometrical or animal shapes are just as fun.
TIP: Store the magnetic letters in a box when not in use.

Clue Zoo

Join your grandkids on a wacky visit to the mixed-up Clue Zoo! Before you leave on a trip, help kids find and cut out large pictures of animals and paste them on poster board. Cut the poster board into strips across the animal bodies in various widths. Mix up the pieces and watch the kids create their new animals!

- For more than one grandchild, give each one a bag of pieces and have kids trade with each other to make their animals.

- Have the kids give you clues about how their new animal would sound or act.

- If kids will be away from home, they can make up a story about their animals to send to their families.

No-Mess Mesh

What is colorful, fun, quiet, and doesn't make a mess? Threading and weaving with mesh! Cut squares of stiff plastic mesh sheeting you purchase from a craft or hobby store. Give kids colored shoelaces or pipe cleaners and they can weave away. TIP: The plastic ends of the shoelaces mean kids don't need to use a needle.

- Draw a pattern on the mesh for the kids to follow.
- Outline an animal on the mesh. Kids can "sew" to match the outline and then weave inside the outline to fill.

Air Travel Tips

Traveling with kids on airplanes presents its own unique challenges, through the often-tedious process of checking in, getting through security, and waiting to board, as well as on the flight itself.

Use a variation of backseat bingo (page 35) to help kids focus while they're waiting for a flight or on the plane. Use words or phrases the kids might hear, rather than see, in the airport or on the plane, such as "captain," "coffee," "exit," or "seat belt" as inspiration for their pictures or stories. Not only are kids more likely to pay attention to announcements and the people around them, but you can also take the opportunity to reassure kids who may be anxious about flying.

WHILE-WE-WAIT ACTIVITY CHAIN

To select fun things to do (that won't disturb your fellow travelers) while you wait in the airport, bring along an activity chain. Cut strips of construction paper of equal lengths to create the links, and write out the activities, such as:

- Walk on your tip-toes for one whole minute – it's harder than your think!

- Identify items in the environment: everything that's red or anything that starts with the letter "s," for example. Use a variety of colors and letters on different links in the chain.

- Count the people who are "____." The choices are endless, such as people who are on their phones, people who are eating something, people who are running, as well as people traveling with kids!

- "Grandma Says" instructions, such as "Grandma says wear your jacket (sweater, etc.) inside out," or "Grandma says touch your toes ten times." The objective is to keep kids moving and active without bothering the people around you.

When you have a number of activities on the paper strips, use tape to close the links into interlocking loops. Let kids work from one end to the other, and watch the time "fly" by!

BUSY BAG PUPPETS

Before you set out on a road trip, have grandkids color paper sandwich bags as people or animals. Fold the bottom of the bag over to make the mouth, and have kids add ears, nose, eyes, and hair with crayons, or bits of fabric or construction paper. Kids can chatter away with their puppets for miles!

WHILE-WE-WAIT WORD SCRAMBLES

Ask the kids to read from one of their favorite books (or yours!) in unusual ways. These are great quiet activities when you are waiting in an airport or at a restaurant, or at the doctor's or dentist's offices, too.

- Kids read just the first word of each line going down the page. What story does this tell?
- Have kids use the first letter of the first word in each line to make as many words as they can from these letters.
- Take turns reading every third word in the book, or every other line.
- Choose a paragraph and ask kids to write down the words it contains in alphabetic order.

Food Adventures!

Whether waiting in a restaurant or grocery shopping with grand-kids, here are ideas to make the time pass and the experience fun.

Opposites Attract Fun!

Most kids develop their dominant-hand tendencies early, which makes this opposites game so engaging. Ask kids to draw or write with the hand they don't normally use. Many restaurants provide coloring pages and crayons, but any type of paper and markers will do.

- Have kids draw with their opposite hands. Suggest objects and topics, or let the kids come up with some on their own.

- Have kids draw an animal with their opposite hands and have everyone else guess what it is.

- Ask kids to write the names of everyone at the table with the opposite hand.

- Have kids write a sentence or phrase of their own and let everyone at the table try to guess what it says!

GRATITUDE AND GRACE

Add time for reflection with your grandkids before the meal by asking them to think of three things they are thankful for. As you all say grace, go around the table and let each child contribute to the prayer.

- Have kids write down their three things on separate slips of paper. Collect the slips in an empty glass and ask whoever leads the prayer to include what's in the glass. TIP: Stash some paper and pencils in your bag beforehand.
- Pass the glass around the table and have others choose a slip to read what the kids are grateful for.

BOX DICE

As a version of Toss the Box in "Boredom Busters" (page16), make smaller boxes as dice to use on a table or counter, such as at a restaurant. Write quiet activities on the sides, such as, "Say the alphabet backwards," and "Count to 10 by 2s."

- Add goofy options sure to bring laughter, such as "Every time someone walks through the door, pat your head for a full minute." "Whenever the server is at your table, lay your head on the shoulder of the person next to you."

- Draw shapes on the sides of the boxes such as circles, diamonds, ovals, squares. Ask kids to identify things around them in these shapes.

Grocery Games

Grocery shopping isn't a chore with your grandkids when you share the sights and smells of the market with them! Pick a letter from the alphabet and have kids take turns naming items they see in the store that start with it. For a long shopping trip, start with "A" and keep going.

- Let kids hold vegetables and produce you put in the cart.

- Show them how to scratch an orange peel for the delightful smell, or feel the difference between a smooth cucumber and a pineapple.

- Have kids write their names or draw on banana peels with a pencil eraser. By the time you get home, their names or drawings will appear on the peel!

- Give kids a job to do – carry items to the cart or count out the carrots.

- Help kids do math at the cash register.

Pasta Super Challenge

The more the merrier for this messy game! Have the players sit around a table and place a bowl of spaghetti in front of each. Each player puts their hands behind their backs and with no silverware the first to finish the bowl of pasta is the winner.

- For a fun variation use a plate instead of a bowl!

Kids Are In The Kitchen with Grandma

We all know everyone likes to hang out in the kitchen and grandkids are no exception. Kids have fun spending time with Grandma, learning to measure and mix, and enjoying their own culinary creations! Share your expertise with your grandkids with these recipes and games.

BLUEBERRY OVERNIGHT OATMEAL RECIPE

When grandkids come to stay over, have them help you make this tasty overnight oatmeal recipe.

Ingredients:
- 1 cup steel cut oats
- 1/4 cup maple syrup or honey
- 2 tsp. vanilla extract
- 2 cups milk
- 2 cups water
- 1 cup blueberries (fresh or frozen)

Add the ingredients to a crock pot and gently stir. Cook for 8-1/2 hours on low (overnight) so the oatmeal will be ready in the morning. Serve with brown sugar, cinnamon, and additional blueberries on top. TIP: You can make the oatmeal without the blueberries in the recipe ... just add them to the top later.

Marshmallow Animals

With big marshmallows and straws, have kids assemble – or create! – their favorite animals. Grandma cuts the straws into various lengths so kids can attach legs, arms, and necks to a marshmallow "body." Cut marshmallows into smaller pieces or use mini marshmallows for the heads. Kids can use food coloring to paint their animals, such as yellow and brown for giraffes, and black for zebra stripes. Push raisins or dried berries into the marshmallow (or stick on with a bit of sunflower butter) for eyes and mouths. Trimmed pipe cleaner pieces work well for ears. If you keep everything edible, when kids are done with their creations, you can always make S'mores!

Finger Gelatin Blocks

Finger gelatin blocks won't melt at room temperature, so make some ahead of time for a special occasion … or just for fun. Think strawberry red for Valentine's Day, lime green for St. Patrick's Day or Christmas, and orange for Thanksgiving. TIP: Make two batches, one red and one blue, for the 4th of July.

You'll need:
- 4 envelopes unflavored gelatin
- 3 packages flavored gelatin (3 ounces each)
- 4 cups boiling water

Add boiling water to the gelatins and pour into ice cube trays. Chill until set. You can also use ice cube trays with shapes such as hearts or flowers!

Fun with Foil

   While you're cooking, give kids some
aluminum foil to make shiny creatures! Cut square pieces of tinfoil
to scrunch or roll up for the bodies, and give kids different lengths
and widths of foil to twist into arms, legs, heads, and tails. Pipe
cleaners are a nice addition for necks, ears, and even antennae!

Milk Sherbert

1 envelope flavored gelatin   1-1/2 cups sugar
3 cups milk   1/2 tsp. salt
2 cups half and half   Food coloring if desired

In a saucepan, Grandma sprinkles the gelatin over 1 cup of the
milk and cooks over low heat, stirring constantly until gelatin is
dissolved. Set aside. In a large bowl, kids can measure and
combine the remaining ingredients with the rest of the milk.
Gradually stir in gelatin mixture. Pour into cake pans or cupcake
tins, with or without paper. Cover with foil and freeze. Serve
with delight!

Walking Water

   Grandkids observe how water travels up … though celery! Place
a stalk of celery in a glass of water mixed with food coloring, and
watch with your grandkids as the colored water makes its way up
the stalk. Best of all, colored celery is great to eat.

Edible (Yes, Edible!) Play Clay

Kids do like playing with modeling clay you buy commercially … but what's even more fun is eating their creations! Create this edible play clay for your grandkids with these common ingredients.

- 1 cup sunflower seed butter
- 1 cup corn syrup
- 1-1/4 cup nonfat dry milk
- 1-1/4 cup confectioner's sugar

With clean hands, kids combine ingredients until thoroughly mixed and then mold away to their hearts' content. Kids can "paint" their creations with food coloring and when they're done, they can also eat their projects!

Grandma S'mores

In the oven, for a crowd: Preheat oven to 400 degrees. Line a baking sheet with parchment paper. Unroll a tube of purchased crescent roll dough onto the paper. Pinch the seams together and fold up the edges of the rectangular sheet of dough to form a short crust. Combine 1-1/2 Tbls. of sugar and 1/2 tsp. of cinnamon in a bowl and sprinkle over the dough. Bake crust 10 to 15 minutes or until golden brown. Remove baking sheet from oven and top with 6 chocolate bars, each 9.3 oz. Cover the bars with one bag of large marshmallows. Return to the oven for about 10 minutes. Watch carefully and remove as soon as the marshmallows melt and turn brown. Cut into 12 pieces and serve!

In the microwave, one at a time: Place 1/2 of a graham cracker on a microwaveable plate. Top with a large square of chocolate and a large marshmallow. Microwave on high 15 to 20 seconds, or until marshmallow puffs. Top with another graham cracker. Let cool for a minute. Eat and enjoy!

MARSHMALLOW CASTLES

A challenge for future engineers! Build a castle – but instead of bricks and boards – use marshmallows and pretzels! Press a marshmallow onto each end of a pretzel. Press pretzels into the sides of those marshmallows and add more pretzels to the marshmallows, going different directions. Form a foundation then keep building up and up as high as you can. Kids can team up on the construction, or have a contest for who can make the tallest or biggest castle.

POTATO PRINT PLAY (NON-EDIBLE)

Grandma cuts a potato in half and pares the potato down around a shape, such as a heart or, if you're feeling ambitious, cut around the child's initials! Have kids paint the shape and press the potato end onto white paper to make a print. Kids can make several prints with the same paint, and you can just repaint the shape when needed to make more.

POTATO PRINT BACKDROPS (NON-EDIBLE)

Another use for your potatoes! Grandma cuts several potatoes in half so kids can paint irregular shapes on the ends in shades of green, for a forest or meadow backdrop. Kids make overlapping prints on white construction paper, and cut pictures of animals, flowers, lakes, etc., out of magazines to paste into their scenes.

Memory, Vocabulary, and Counting Games

Kids never stop learning ... and games with Grandma help kids with critical thinking, decision making, vocabulary, counting and math, and memory. Here are some of our favorites.

Two-Word Rhymes

Ask kids to make up 2-word rhymes, such as "ouch couch," "floor snore," or "supermoon bedroom." They don't have to make sense, and the sillier they are, the more fun everyone has!

First Letter, Last Letter

Get kids started with a word such as "red." The next player needs to use a word that starts with the last letter of the previous word, such as "downstairs" for the "d" in red. Continue this word chain with all the kids as long as you can!

RE**D** ⟶ **D**OWNSTAIRS

First-Letter Quiz

Kids love their names – most do, anyway. Here's an interesting way to have fun with names, especially when you are waiting in line, at the doctor's office, or at a restaurant. For each of these topics, ask kids to come up with answers starting with the first letters of their names. For example, Rory might answer "ravioli" for a food. TIP: Play a round using the first letters of their middle names, too!

You can use any topic, and kids of different ages can help the younger ones. Grandkids will love it if you play, too!

Rory

- Color   Red
- Animal   Raccoon
- City or state   Rhode Island
- Flower   Rose
- Food   Ravioli
- Cartoon character?   Robin Hood
- A word that starts and end with the same letter   ROAR
- Girl's name   Rachel
- Boy's name   Ryder

I Spy ...

For this memory game, Grandma arranges an even number of paper plates (at least 8...or make it super hard and use 20!) on the counter or table, and writes 2 each of letters, numbers, or colors on individual sticky notes, placing 1 underneath each plate. Kids take turns flipping over 2 plates at a time to try to find a match.

Arts & Crafts

Extraordinary Ideas with Ordinary Things

If you have an odds-and-ends drawer or pieces of fabric folded away, you and your grandkids can make extraordinary creations from these everyday items.

SHELL PAINTING

Many kids know how to paint rocks, but have they painted shells? Purchase large shells at hobby or craft stores, and let kids paint the inside and outside of the shells. Kids can add yarn, flowers, fabric, or whatever scraps you have handy!

- To make shell people, help kids attach their painted shells to poster board or construction paper. Once the paint dries, kids can draw faces with markers on the shells and color in the bodies. Add more nature to this craft and have kids use twigs for the arms and legs.

Building Beautiful Butterflies

Few things are more entrancing than butterflies! Although grandkids do enjoy chasing real butterflies that flitter around the yard, kids can also build their own butterflies with a few simple materials.

Pipe Cleaner Butterflies

Kids use pipe cleaners to twist around colorful tissue paper for butterfly bodies. Help kids trim shorter lengths of pipe cleaners to attach as antennae. TIP: Sheer fabric dipped in liquid starch and dried makes perfect – and more permanent – wings.

Clothespin Butterflies

Plain wooden clothespins make wonderful butterfly bodies (although plastic pins work just as well) and kids can use markers or paint to color their clothespins. Help cut squares of tissue paper or use short lengths of crepe paper streamers and clamp them in the middle with the clothespins. Trim pipe cleaners and have kids glue them to the butterfly bodies as antennae.

WATERCOLOR BUTTERFLIES

For stunning watercolor butterflies, you'll need flat-bottomed white coffee filters, markers, and a few glasses of water. Cover a table or counter with newspaper to protect the surface. Flatten the coffee filters on the newspaper, and draw a circle around the center of the filter with a non-permanent marker, using different colors for different filters. Close the coffee filters into a cone shape by folding them in half and then in half again. Position the cones over glasses of water, spreading out the top of the filters, so that the tip touches the water, making sure the colored marker circle doesn't reach the water.

Kids can watch as the filter absorbs water that travels up through the colored circle to the edge, drawing the color through the wings." Place the filters flat on the newspaper and, when dry, scrunch up the middle and wrap a pipe cleaner around the center for the body. Trim pipe cleaners into shorter lengths and twist around the butterfly bodies as antennae. TIP: Clothespins make great bodies for watercolor butterflies, too.

Piñata Memory Capsule

Here's a twist on the traditional time capsule that's even more fun at the end! Make a piñata memory capsule to stash away memories and mementos from one year to the next.

You'll need:
- Newspapers
- Paper towels
- Flour
- Water
- Paint
- White glue, thinned with water

- Thin plastic inflatible beach ball
- String, ribbon, or rope
- Crepe paper streamers or paper fringe garlands from a local craft or party store

1. Inflate the beach ball to about 20 inches. Kids can make paper mâché glue by mixing one part flour with one part water to the consistency of heavy cream, stirring until there are no lumps.

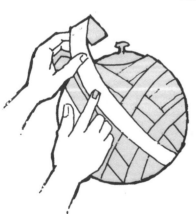

2. Have kids rip the newspaper into strips about an inch in width and then dip into the paper mâché glue mix. Wipe off excess glue, and layer the newspaper strips on the ball. Leave a circle of 4 inches wide around the air stopper plug of the bag, so you can remove the ball and fill your memory capsule later.

3. Repeat with the newspaper strips until you have three or four layers of paper mâché. Add strips of paper towels as a last layer for a white surface. Let the piñata dry overnight so kids can paint on the outside of the memory capsule. Finish by brushing on a thin layer of glue mixture (2/3 glue to 1/3 water) to preserve the paintings.

4. Deflate the ball and pull it carefully through the opening, then help kids fill the capsule with drawings, notes, photographs, or small non-fragile toys that are important to them. Ask your grandkids why they want to remember these items as you add them to the capsule.

5. Decorate the top of the capsule with crepe paper streamers or fringe garland to hide the hole.

6. Decide with your grandkids on a length of time before they will open the memory capsule. Store it somewhere the kids will see it when they visit as a reminder of what they can look forward to.

7. When kids are ready to open the capsule, Grandma uses any utensil to make two holes through the top near the opening. Thread a shoe lace through the holes and tie off to hang the piñata somewhere kids can whack at it with a foam bat. Enjoy reliving memories with your grandkids as they rediscover all the treasures that fall out!

GUMDROP TREES

Gumdrop trees are great to have or make as gifts for Christmas, and provide a great opportunity to talk with your grandkids about the reason for the season. TIP: Gumdrop trees are not only fun at the holidays, but any time of year! NOTE: The gumdrops are not edible after they're used in these crafts.

- Have kids use a small branch with several "arms" for the tree, and remove any leaves. Kids can paint the tree brown or green, and paint a paper or plastic cup white for the stand. Push the bottom of the "tree" into a gumdrop, and stand it up on the bottom of the cup. Fill around the tree with sand, clay, or cornmeal so it stands upright. Kids stick a gumdrop on each end of each branch as leaves or Christmas ornaments!

- Purchase green cone-shaped pieces of florist's foam in different sizes from a craft store. Help kids push one end of a toothpick into the bottom of the gumdrops and attach to the tree with the other end. Use different colors for the ornaments and lights!

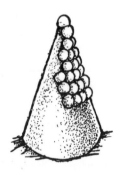

PULLED STRING PAINTING

Simple string, paper, and paint combine for amazing art!

You'll need:

- Paper
- String or yarn
- Tempera or activity paint
- Small containers for paint cups

Fill the cups with paint, and have kids coat the string or yarn by dipping it into a paint cup. Kids lay the strings anywhere on the paper and drag, swirl, or wiggle the string all around to create the artwork. Use lots of different colors and mix them up on the paper with various strings. (Let each color dry before adding another or the painting may turn muddy brown.)

- Kids can use various lengths of string to create circles and swirls.
- Have kids fold the paper in half and pull several strings through in any direction. Open the paper to reveal the creation!

More ways to use your string masterpiece!

While the paint is still wet, add texture by pressing into it using a cotton ball, sponge, paintbrush – even a toy car! Experiment with the textures created by different objects.

After the paint is dry, kids can cut the string art into fun shapes such as leaves, hearts, stars, people, etc. Use these cut outs to make a collage by gluing onto heavy paper or another art piece.

Use string art designs to make fun borders for framing pictures of family and friends.

KIDS-INSIDE PHOTO BOOK

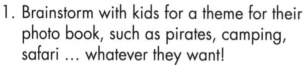

Not only will kids enjoy making this book with Grandma, but they'll come back to it over and over again!

1. Brainstorm with kids for a theme for their photo book, such as pirates, camping, safari ... whatever they want!
2. Help kids locate and cut out pictures from magazines that fit their theme.
3. For the back cover, cut poster board into a 7-inch square.
4. Have grandkids cut out photos of their faces in ovals about 1-1/4 inch wide and 1-3/4 inch high. Paste the pictures onto the inside of the back covers about in the center of the square.
5. Cut several pieces of construction paper or drawing paper to 7-inch squares, and carefully cut holes in each page in the same position as the photo on the inside back cover, so that the photo shows through all the pages. TIP: Grandma should cut out the ovals on the pages!
6. Cut another square of the poster board for the front cover, and make a hole for the photo to show through.
7. Following their themes, kids draw their bodies and scenes around their photo on all the pages and add images they cut out.
8. Have kids draw on the front cover, and add a title such as "_____ Goes on Safari!" or "_____, the Pirate!"
9. Kids write their names and the date on the outside back cover of the book.
10. Grandma helps kids bind their books with staples, spiral binding, or other bookbinding techniques.

Take Time for Quiet Time

Grandkids enjoy a cool Grandma, but they also treasure quiet time with you, talking together, playing simple games, and snuggling close.

WHAT DO WE DO WELL?

If you're entertaining more than one grandchild, ask them to say a few things about one another that each person does well ... sing, play marbles, tell jokes. Give them thought starters such as, "I think you are good at ___" or "I like the way you _____." TIP: Oversee this game to make sure the observations are kind! Afterward, take a moment to give thanks for the unique abilities of each child.

THINGS WE LIKE TO DO

Talk with your grandkids about what they like to do, such as take a walk, cook with Grandma, visit the library, kick balls in the park ... anything you can share together. Help kids create a chart with boxes where they can draw, paint, or color these activities. Have kids place stickers on the chart after enjoying the activity with Grandma! TIP: This is also a great travel game. Have grandkids draw and color activities they can expect at their destination.

Love Map Heart

Help kids draw a large heart on poster board or cut one out of construction paper and paste to the board. Ask your grandchildren what's in their hearts ... who they love, what they are thankful for, what they look forward to. Jot down their answers on the Love Map heart, or have kids write and draw them. Bring out the love maps from time to time and spend a few quiet minutes talking with your grandchildren about what's in their hearts.

- For a powerful gift, have kids fold up their Love Map hearts and put into an envelope for Father's or Mother's Day.

Hand Shadow Puppets

All you need is a blank wall, a light, and some hands when it's time for an after-dinner activity, or when winding down at bedtime. Show kids how to make and move shadow animals just by changing your hands. A good light source is a heavy duty flashlight or flexible neck lamp that can be directed at the wall. Have kids experiment with what happens when their hands are close to the light (the shadow is larger but not as crisp) and when their hands are further from the light (the shadow is smaller but clearer). Now watch their shadow animals come to life! TIP: You can use a wall, screen, or white sheet for the background.

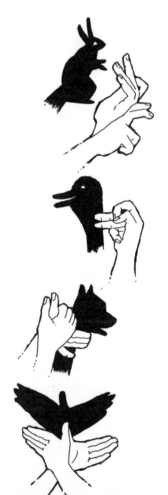

Zipper Mood Meter: How do I feel today?

Kids are often asked to use faces – a smiley face, a frowny face – to let us know how they're feeling. Use this zipper mood meter to talk with grandkids about what's going on with them.

- Glue or tape the zipper securely to poster board. Use a permanent marker to draw a smiley face on the poster board next to the top of the zipper. Draw a frowny face on the poster board next to the bottom of the zipper. Kids can quickly locate their moods, with the added benefit of letting them position the zippers between the two. TIP: You can also draw faces with expressions that indicate different emotions (angry, excited) along the sides the zippers.

- Older kids can use what they know about how numbers relate to each other. With a permanent marker, write ascending numbers on the zippers, beginning with "1" at the bottom and ending with "10" at the top. Explain that 1 means unhappy and 10 means happy, and ask them to zip the zippers to the numbers closest to their moods.

For either mood meter game, be sure to ask if kids are feeling happy or unhappy. Follow up with questions such as "Why are you feeling sad right now?" and "What would make you feel better?"

P.S. Don't forget to ask, "What is making you so happy today?" if kids zip high on the mood meter!

Games For a Group

Although both Grandma and grandkids enjoy spending time one on one, sometimes a whole group of kids is extra fun! Here are some of our favorite group activities that could also be scaled down for only one or two kids.

PIRATES PLUNDER!

What kids don't like pirates? Play this game with up to 8 people of all ages … young children are able to easily grasp the idea.

You will need…

- 2 decks of cards, shuffled together
- Dice
- Pirates Plunder Bag for each player

Prepare the Game:

- Put 30 items – assorted types of candy, toys, coins, etc., anything small that will fit inside individual games bags.

- Remove all face cards from the deck and set aside. Give each player a secret Pirates Plunder Bag. Kids can look inside but not take anything out.

Instructions:

1. Deal 10 cards to each player. Kids place the cards on the table in front of them, face up so they can see the numbers on each card.

2. Give the dice to the player who will start the game and move the dice in subsequent turns around the table to the left.

3. The first player rolls the dice. Players review their cards laid in front of them, and if any players have cards with the number rolled, they discard the cards in the center of the table. For example, if a 4 is rolled, players discard all 4s in their hands.

4. However, any players who do not have a card matching that number must take that number of items from their Pirates Plunder Bag and place them on the table next to the discarded cards.

5. The dice move to the next player for another turn.

6. The center stash of Pirates Plunder grows until any player rolls an 11 or 12, and that player gets all the Plunder in the center!

7. Note: Even when players have no items left in their bag, they still roll the dice. If they have the rolled number, they discard the card. If not, the dice pass to the next player. If the current player rolls 11 or 12, they get the Plunder!

8. The game continues until one player has no cards left in front of them and they get any Pirates Plunder still remaining on the table. The final winner is the player who has the most Plunder!

Am I smaller than a dog?

"What-Am-I?" Headbands

Make index cards ahead of time by cutting out different pictures such as animals, objects, people, plants from a catalog or a magazine to paste on the cards. Give grandkids each a card, face down so they don't see what's on it. Sitting in a circle, kids tuck their cards, face out, into stretchy headbands.(No peeking!) Each takes a turn asking the others a yes/no question. Go around the circle, one question at a time as kids try to figure out who or what is pictured on their forehead!

Grandma's Treasure Hunt!

With a little preparation, Grandma can create a treasure hunt the grandkids are sure to remember!

- Write clues on paper and hide them far apart in places that aren't similar to each other.
- Choose locations kids are familiar with, such as inside a pillowcase, taped under the kitchen table, inside a musical instrument, behind the television.
- Fill the "Treasure Box" (a decorated shoe box will work fine) with special small items your grandchildren will enjoy.
- Give kids bags or envelopes to collect their clues. Take them to clue #1 and send them on the treasure hunt!

Here are some clues we like – adapt as you need for your own Treasure Hunt!

Clue #1 for Clue #2:
Draw a picture of Grandma's shoe on the clue. "The fun has begun with Clue #1 ... peek into Grandma's shoe for Treasure Hunt Clue #2!"

Clue #2 for Clue #3:
Put Clue #3 in a small envelope, then a bigger one, then a bigger one, wrap them all in tape and place under the chair. "It's Clue #2 so here's what you do: Look under Grandma's chair to see if Clue #3 hides there."

Clue #3 for Clue #4:
Place some cutout footprints leading around the kitchen floor to Clue #4. "From Clue #3, now what do you see? Is that Clue #4 on Grandma's kitchen floor?"

Clue #4 for Clue #5:
Mix up the letters for PILLOW-CASE – such as CAPSOWLELI – on the bottom of Clue #4. "After Clue #4 look past the bedroom door and check around just in case Clue #5 is in this place!"

Clue #5 for Clue #6:
Have some bath beads or a bar of soap inside the pillowcase to lead kids to the bathtub. "Now Clue #5 wants you to arrive at your Clue #6 where there's water to mix!"

Clue #6 for Clue #7:
Cut out pictures of various musical instruments – including those you don't have – that kids can look for. TIP: If you don't own one, use a radio or stereo! "Does Clue #6 say that music's the way your Clue #7 is found? Take your time and look around!"

Clue #7 for Treasure:
Draw a "map" on this clue that will lead kids through the house or yard to the Treasure! "#7 is your final clue and all that you do is give your hands a clap and follow the Treasure Hunt map!"

Treasure: Have a few items, such as shiny coins, outside the Treasure Box! "Good for you! Now give a cheer ... Your Treasure is here!"

Punch-Out Cards, Games, & Puzzles

Included in this book are unique cards and game pieces, perforated for you to punch out. Cards are printed front AND back, providing over 20 different games to play.

To keep it simple, we recommend you sort and store games in separate zip-top bags between play.

Instructions for all these games follow!:

1. Bible Story Bingo
2. Slime Out!
3. Go Dig! Treasure Hunt Game
4. Wild Ones!
5. Pick-a-Pair!
6. Name Game
7. Silly Character Name Game
8. Match the Jax!
9. Noah's Ark Puzzle
10. Noah's Ark-Find the Hidden Objects
11. Neighborhood Scavenger Hunt
12. Travel Scavenger Hunt
13. Around-the-House Scavenger Hunt
14. Take a Hike Scavenger Hunt
15. Lady Bug-Match Two
16. Spotted Pony-Match the Spots
17. Mountain Maze
18. Ancient City Maze
19. Wild Journey Maze
20. "What's Different?" Under the Sea Puzzle
21. "What's Different?" Lightning Puzzle

BIBLE STORY BINGO

NUMBER OF PLAYERS:
• 2 to 10

NUMBER OF CARDS:
• 1 BINGO CARD EACH

OBJECT OF GAME:
Be the first player to form a straight line of 5 markers on the BINGO card, either horizontally, vertically, or diagonally.

GAME PIECES INCLUDED:
• 10 BINGO cards • 1 Caller Card • 70 Call pieces
(Store in a zip-top plastic bag after playing.)

YOU WILL ALSO NEED:
Coins, buttons, candies, or other items to use as markers.

SET UP:
Each player receives a BINGO card which they lay in front of them along with their pile of markers. Place one marker in the center space of the BINGO card. One person is designated the "Caller" and is given the caller card, the small pieces sorted by the letters in one pile and the pictures in another.

Example: "G-Lamb!"

PLAY:
When a letter-picture combination is called, the picture marker is placed on the right spot on the caller card. The letter piece called is returned and mixed up in the letter pile. Each player seeks to locate that combination on their card and find it, place a marker on the space. Each combination is called only once. The first person to place 5 markers in a straight line calls "BINGO!" The "winner" then calls back their combinations to the Caller, who compares it to the Caller card. If all match, the person wins. If a combination is read that is not on the Caller card, the game continues until a player has an authentic BINGO.

Slime Out!

NUMBER OF PLAYERS:

• 2 or more

NUMBER OF CARDS:

• 44 FACE CARDS **+**
  1 SLIME OUT CARD
  (DO NOT INCLUDE
  "WILD" CARDS.)

THIS GAME WILL FOCUS ON:

• NUMBERS ONLY ————————▶

1, 2, 3, 4, 5, 6, 7, 8, 9, 10, 11

OBJECTIVE:

• Players try to get rid of all the cards in their hands
  before their opponents do by drawing from their
  opponent's hands and discarding *pairs*.
  (If you have 3 cards with the same number, one of
  them stays in your hand!) The player left with the Slime Out card loses and
  everyone cheers "Slime Out!"

• How to make the loser a winner? Make up a batch of "Slime"
  (recipe is on the next page) and give the loser the Slime prize!

PLAYING THE GAME:

• Deal all cards. Players sort through their cards, making as many pairs as
  possible, and placing these pairs face-up on the table in front of them.
  The remaining stay in players hands, hidden from other players.

PLAYING THE GAME, CONTINUED:

• Starting with the dealer, each player then takes a turn fanning out the cards in their hands face down so the player to their left can draw one card. The player is not allowed to see the other player's hand. Play continues as players make pairs in their hands, they lay them out face up immediately on the table. The first player to run out of cards wins. The loser is the player with the Slime Out card.

CHANGE THE GAME:

• See how the game changes if you decide the winner is the person left with the "Slime Out!" card! It's a challenge to hang on to the Slime Out card instead of getting rid of it.

"SLIME" RECIPE:

Slime is a weird substance that has the properties of both liquids and solids. You can put your hand in Slime just like you can dip your hand in water. But you can also shape the slime into a ball. Here's an easy recipe for you and the kids to make this weird slimy stuff.

You will need:
• 2 cups of cornstarch   • Bowl
• 1 cup of water   • Green food coloring (optional)

Step 1: Combine the cornstarch and water in the bowl.
Step 2: Have the kids mix the ingredients together with their hands until you have slime!

If your slime is too watery, add a little more cornstarch. If it is too stiff, add a little more water. You can also add food coloring if you want to make colored slime.

Go Dig! The Treasure Hunt Game

NUMBER OF PLAYERS:

• 2 or more

NUMBER OF CARDS:

• 44 FACE CARDS (DO NOT INCLUDE "SLIME OUT!" OR "WILD" CARDS.)

THIS GAME WILL FOCUS ON:

• NUMBERS ONLY ⟶

1, 2, 3, 4, 5, 6, 7, 8, 9, 10, 11

PLAYING THE GAME:

• Deal cards face down to the players.
• For 2 to 3 players, deal each player 7 cards.
• If there are more than three players, deal 5 cards each.
• Spread the rest of the deck out in the middle of the players face down. This is the "Dirt Pile."
• The objective is to get a set of 4 matching numbers that kids place down in front of them during your turn.

TAKING A TURN:

• The player to the left of the dealer starts the game and then turns move clockwise from there.

• During a turn, the player tells another player they are hunting for a particular number on a card. For example, player 1 may say to player 2: "I'm hunting for nines." If Player 2 has any nines, they must give all of his nines to player 1. If player 2 doesn't have any nines, they say "Go Dig!"

TAKING A TURN, CONTINUED:

- When you "Go Dig!" you choose one card from the "Dirt Pile."

- If the player gets the card(s) they asked for, either from the Dirt Pile or from Player 2, Player 1 gets another turn. During a turn, if they get four of the same number, they put the cards face up in front of them. For example, if a player already had 3 nines, then picked up another nine from the Dirt Pile, they get to place the set of 4 cards down and get another turn.

WINNING THE GAME:

- "Go Dig!" is over when one player runs out of cards or there are no more cards in the "Dirt Pile." The winner is determined by who has the most sets of cards in front of them. If two players have the same number of sets, the player with the higher values is the winner.

"GO DIG!" STRATEGY:

- Players try to memorize what cards the other players have and want.

- If they pick up a card number from the "Dirt Pile" that they didn't have, it's good to guess that number on the next turn.

- Try to "Go Dig!" more at the start of the game. This gets players more cards and a better chance of getting more matches later.

ALTERNATIVE WAYS TO PLAY "GO DIG!":

Mix things up, try these other ways to play the game:

- At the end of the game, deduct a point for each card a player is holding. This way, players have a balance between wanting a lot of cards to get matches and getting rid of their cards before the end of the game.

- Try playing to get pairs of cards instead of sets of four.

WILD ONES CARD GAME

NUMBER OF PLAYERS:

• 2 to 4

NUMBER OF CARDS:

• 44 FACE CARDS
(DO NOT INCLUDE
"SLIME OUT!" OR
"WILD" CARDS.)

**THIS GAME WILL
FOCUS ON:**

• SHAPES ◆ ♥ ● ★
• NUMBERS

1, 2, 3, 4, 5, 6, 7, 8, 9, 10, 11

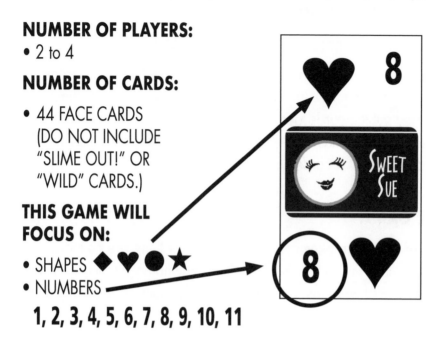

PLAYING THE GAME:

• Deal 5 cards face down to the players.

• The remaining cards go in a stack face down in the middle.
Turn the top card over beside the stack to start the discard pile.

• During a player's turn, they can play a single card, face up on the discard
pile, that matches the current card in either shape such as a heart, or number.
For example, if the current face card is the 5 of hearts, they may play either
a 5 or a heart.

• Number 1s are wild and can be played instead of a match. When a player
plays a 1, they get to state what they want the new shape to be, such as,
hearts, stars, circles, or diamonds.

• If the player can't match the top card they must draw cards from the
deck until they get a match. Players can stop after drawing three cards. When
the draw pile is empty, players that don't have a match lose their turn.

WINNING THE GAME:

- The first player to discard all their cards is the winner! If all players still have cards left, and no one has a match to play, the winner is the player with the fewest cards or the lowest value (you decide).

STRATEGIES FOR "WILD ONES":

- If players play a 1, they can either choose the shape that they have the most of or can pick one they think their opponent doesn't have (if you can remember what shape they last had to draw a card for).

- If playing for points (adding up card values at the end of each round), players should play the high cards first when matching a shape, because the winner will be the player with the lowest points when one player has reached 100 points.

PICK-A-PAIR!

Pick-a-Pair is a good game to play with children of varying ages as young kids can often compete with older ones. It can also be used by one player, playing a "solitary" game of memory challenge.

NUMBER OF PLAYERS:

• 1 or more

NUMBER OF CARDS:

• 44 FACE CARDS (DO NOT INCLUDE "SLIME OUT!" OR "WILD" CARDS.)

THIS GAME WILL FOCUS ON:

• NUMBERS ONLY ⟶

1, 2, 3, 4, 5, 6, 7, 8, 9, 10, 11

PLAYING THE GAME:

• To set up a game of "Pick-a-Pair," shuffle the cards and place each card face down. Note: the backs of these game cards have the "Name Game," "Happy Jax," and "Noah's Ark" puzzle pieces. Disregard these sides while playing "Pick-a-Pair."

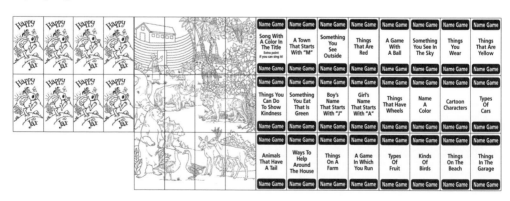

TAKING A TURN:

- Each player takes a turn by flipping two cards over. If the card numbers match, the player picks up the cards and keeps them. If they don't match, the player turns the cards back over. If the player gets a match, they take another turn until they fail to get a match.

- The game is over when all of the cards have been matched and picked up.

WINNING THE GAME:

- The winner of the game is the player with the most matches after all the cards have been picked up.

"PICK-A-PAIR" STRATEGY:

- A good strategy for "Pick-a-Pair" is not to turn over the card players are sure of first. For example, if a player knows exactly where a 2 is, but not sure where the second 2 is, turn over the guess first. If players are wrong, you can then pick a random card and have a chance of getting a match.

ALTERNATIVE WAYS TO PLAY PICK-A-PAIR:

- Stop each turn after only one flip of the cards.

- Add in the 3 Wild Cards from the card deck, which make any card turned over into a match. There will likely be unmatched cards left on the table at the end.

- Kids can play "Pick-a-Pair" by themselves and time the game to complete it faster than before. Or they can try to finish the game in fewer and fewer turns.

Name Games

NAME GAME #1

NUMBER OF PLAYERS:
• 2 or more

NUMBER OF CARDS:
• 28 NAME GAME CARDS

THIS GAME WILL FOCUS ON:
• THE QUESTION ON THE CARD

PLAYING THE GAME:

• Players draw a card and answer the question. Kids can play this as a contest, with players writing the names of answers down to see who gets the most or as a team game, answering back and forth to see how long they can keep the "volley" going.

ALTERNATIVE:

• Kids can play this wherever they are...while waiting in line, sitting in a restuarant, riding in a car, etc. Tip: kids can create their own cards, or make up topics.

NAME GAME #2

NUMBER OF PLAYERS:

- 2 or more

NUMBER OF CARDS:

- 28 NAME GAME CARDS **+**
  SILLY FACES AND VOICES CARDS
  (remaining 20 face cards)

THIS GAME WILL FOCUS ON:

- THE QUESTION ON THE CARD
- THE SILLY FACE CARDS
  (Sweet Sue, Baby Boo, Grouchy Gus,
  Goofy Gilbert)

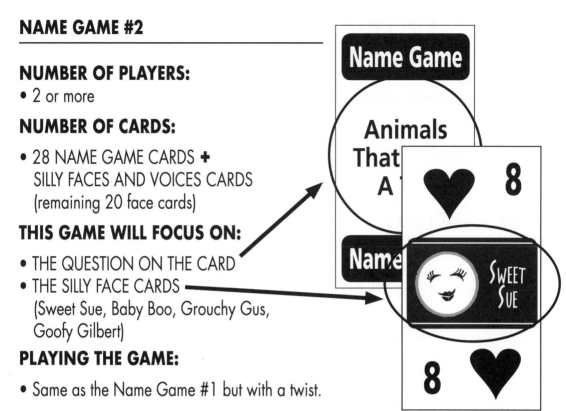

PLAYING THE GAME:

- Same as the Name Game #1 but with a twist.

THE GAME TWIST:

- Put all the Name Game cards in one drawing pile. Use all the remaining face cards with faces down, as a separate draw pool. Kids draw the Name Game card and draw a face card. When players answer the Name Game card they must do it in the voice of the face card character! What would Grouchy Gus sounds like? Or Baby Boo? Sweet Sue? Goofy Gilbert? (Grandma can help give examples of what a voice may sound like.) Prepare for loads of laughter as kids practice their voices!

ADD ANOTHER ELEMENT:

- When kids draw the face card, they must answer in the voice AND answer the name question with the number that is on the back of the "Name Game" card: For example, kids must name 8 animals that have a tail in the voice of Sweet Sue. If they don't, another person gets to try and if they succeed in naming the full number of answers (8), they get the score!

NOAH'S ARK HIDDEN PUZZLE

NUMBER OF PLAYERS:

• 1 or more

NUMBER OF CARDS:

• 12 PUZZLE CARDS

OBJECT OF GAME:

Arrange the 12 puzzle cards in the proper place to form the scene of Noah's Ark. Multiple players take turns drawing a card and placing it where it might fit. Everyone wins when the puzzle is solved. Or, make a set of puzzle cards for each player, and the winner is the first to solve it.

HIDDEN IMAGES GAME:

When the picture is completed, find the images hidden in the scene! For multiple players, see who can find the images the fastest.

(The shaded areas above shown the locations.)

See if you can find:

Pencil

Slice of pizza

Sock

Comb

Baseball cap

Flashlight

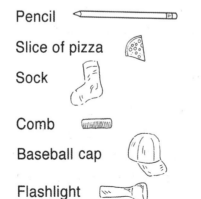

Scissors

Ice cream cone

Crown

Violin

Spoon

Scavenger Hunt Game

NUMBER OF PLAYERS:

• 2 or more

NUMBER OF CARDS:

• 1 CARD PER GAME

OBJECT OF GAME:

To spot all the items on the card.

GAME PIECES INCLUDED:

• 4 Scavenger Hunt Cards

PLAYING THE GAME:

Players find and mark off the items located on the cards. Punch out the 4 scavenger hunt cards, and choose the game that's right for the situation: Travel Scavenger Hunt for the car, Around-the-House Scavenger Hunt when you're in the house, Neighborhood Scavenger Hunt for playing in the yard, and Take a Hike Scavenger Hunt. Make copies, so all players have their own cards.

Neighborhood Scavenger Hunt

MAILBOX · GARBAGE CAN · BASKETBALL HOOP · TREE · FLAG · FLOWER · DOGHOUSE · COOKER · SWING · BENCH · BIRDHOUSE · SLIDE

PHOTOCOPY THIS PAGE FOR MULTIPLE USES.

(Note: To play Scavenger Hunt games more than once, make multiple copies before using.)

WINNING THE GAME:

Players check the box next to the picture of an object they find on their hunt. To reuse the Scavenger Hunt cards, mark lightly with erasable pencil, or place a marker such as a repositionable sticker on the picture. The first player to spot all the items on the card wins.

ALTERNATIVE:

• In addition to the item on the card, see if kids can find things related to that item, such as a mailbox, mail carrier, mail truck, etc.

MATCH THE JAX!

NUMBER OF PLAYERS:
• 1 or more

NUMBER OF CARDS:
• 8 JAX CARDS

OBJECT OF GAME:
Kids meet our special furry pal, Jax!
Arrange the 8 cards in front of them and
look closely! Only two of the cards
are EXACTLY the same. See how quickly
kids can find the two matching JAX cards.

Tail Direction
Flower Direction
Butterfly Direction

(Grandma hint: This is the card
that has a match. Look for the
matches with the arrows.)

MORE BACK-OF-BINGO CARD GAMES! (AND HERE ARE THE ANSWERS...)

Mountain Maze

Wild Journey Maze

Ancient City Maze

Spotted Pony

Lady Bug - Match Two

Lightning Differences:
1. Pull cord on lamp moved.
2. Cuff button removed. 3. Spot
added to dog. 4. Picture frame is
smaller. 5. Pants are colored.
6. Lightning bolt is smaller 7. Plant
added in bottom of window.
8. Tongue added to dog. 9. Pillow
missing on chair.

Undersea Differences: 1. Lobster's eyes are bigger.
2. Lobster claw is open. 3. Top fish switched direction.
4. Spots on two fish removed. 5. Clam's eyes moved.
6. Sea plant on right has been darkened. 7. Single fish
in center is smaller. 8. Air bubbles by lobster are gone.
9. Coral on left shorter. 10. Starfish is smaller.
11. Rock added under lobster claw. 12. Jellyfish is
smaller. 13. Tiny fish added above lobster.

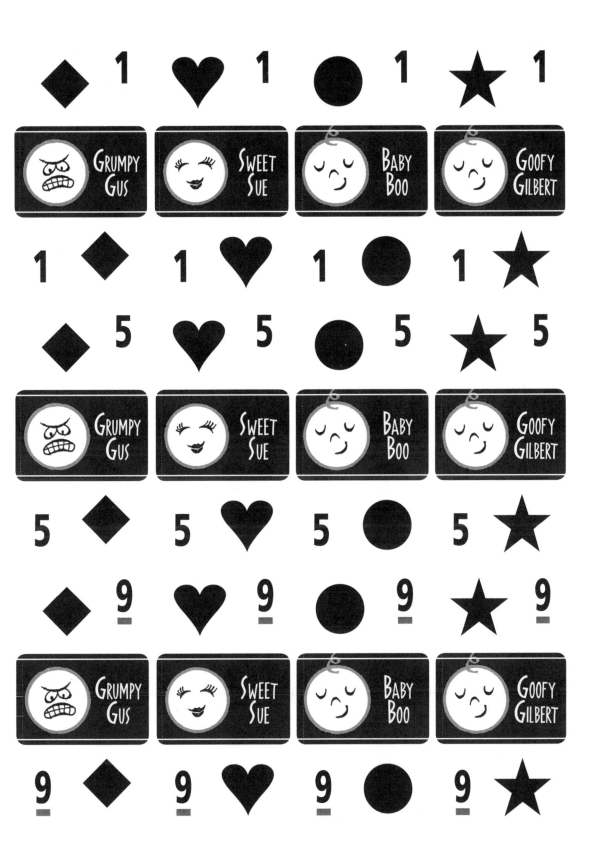

| **Name Game** | **Name Game** | **Name Game** | **Name Game** |

| A Game
With
A Ball | Something
You See In
The Sky | Things
You
Wear | Things
That Are
Yellow |

| **Name Game** | **Name Game** | **Name Game** | **Name Game** |
| **Name Game** | **Name Game** | **Name Game** | **Name Game** |

| Things
That Have
Wheels | Name
A
Color | Cartoon
Characters | Types
Of
Cars |

| **Name Game** | **Name Game** | **Name Game** | **Name Game** |
| **Name Game** | **Name Game** | **Name Game** | **Name Game** |

| Types
Of
Fruit | Kinds
Of
Birds | Things
On The
Beach | Things
In The
Garage |

| **Name Game** | **Name Game** | **Name Game** | **Name Game** |

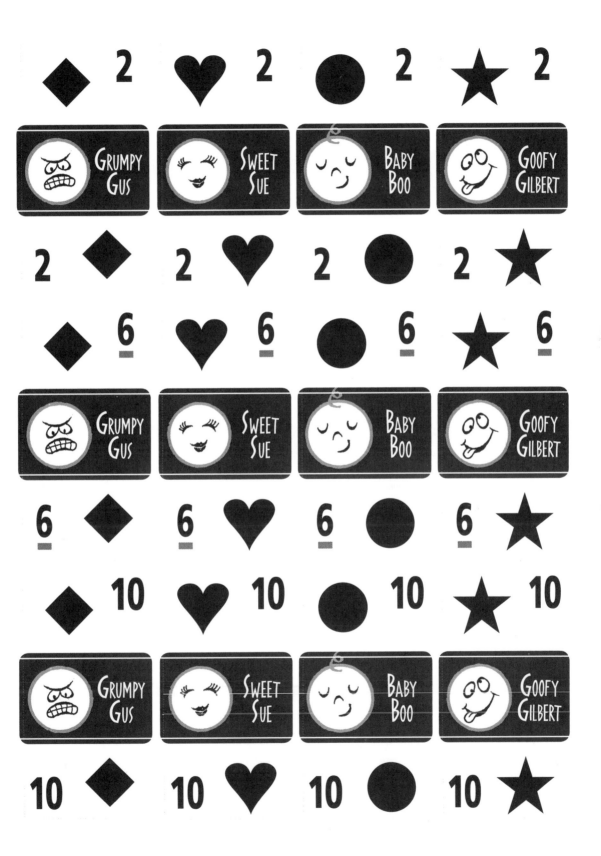

Name Game	**Name Game**	**Name Game**	**Name Game**
Song With A Color In The Title **Extra point if you can sing it!**	A Town That Starts With "M"	Something You See Outside	Things That Are Red

Name Game	**Name Game**	**Name Game**	**Name Game**
Name Game	**Name Game**	**Name Game**	**Name Game**
Things You Can Do To Show Kindness	Something You Eat That Is Green	Boy's Name That Starts With "J"	Girl's Name That Starts With "A"

Name Game	**Name Game**	**Name Game**	**Name Game**
Name Game	**Name Game**	**Name Game**	**Name Game**
Animals That Have A Tail	Ways To Help Around The House	Things On A Farm	A Game In Which You Run
Name Game	**Name Game**	**Name Game**	**Name Game**

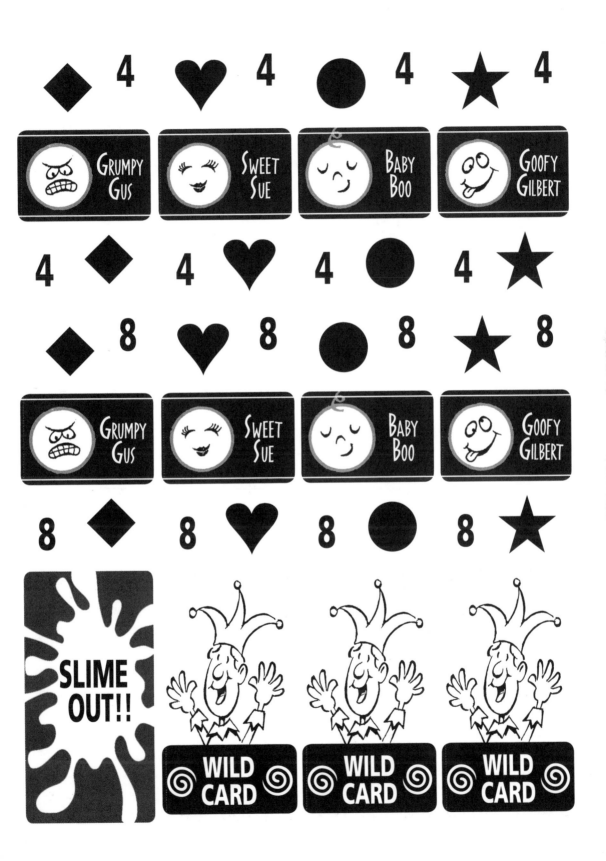

Name Game

Things
That Start
With "B"

Things
That Rhyme
With
"NOT"

Things
That Are
Round

Foods
That Are
"Icky"

Name Game **Name Game** **Name Game** **Name Game**

BIBLE STORY BINGO

Card 1:

PALM	SWORD	HEART	CANDLE	PRAYER
MANGER	SHIELD	WHALE	VESSEL	HARP
HELMET	DOVE	FREE SPACE	LION	BOAT
CAMEL	STAR	BREAD	DONKEY	BIBLE
CHURCH	FISH	DOVE	LAMB	CROWN

Card 2:

ARK	HEART	ANGEL	PALM	CANDLE
SHIELD	WHALE	HARP	MANGER	VESSEL
DOVE	BOAT	FREE SPACE	HELMET	LION
STAR	BREAD	BIBLE	CAMEL	DONKEY
FISH	DOVE	CROWN	CHURCH	LAMB

Neighborhood Scavenger Hunt

 MAILBOX ☐

 BASKETBALL HOOP ☐

 FLAG ☐

 DOGHOUSE ☐

 SWING ☐

 BIRDHOUSE ☐

 GARBAGE CAN ☐

 TREE ☐

 FLOWER ☐

 COOKER ☐

 BENCH ☐

 SLIDE ☐

PHOTOCOPY THIS PAGE FOR MULTIPLE USES.

Take A Hike Scavenger Hunt

 BIRD ☐

 SPIDER ☐

 PINECONE ☐

 FLOWER ☐

 BUTTERFLY ☐

 LADYBUG ☐

 WORM ☐

 PAW PRINT ☐

 LEAF ☐

 ACORN ☐

 MUSHROOM ☐

 TWIG ☐

PHOTOCOPY THIS PAGE FOR MULTIPLE USES.

BIBLE STORY

BINGO

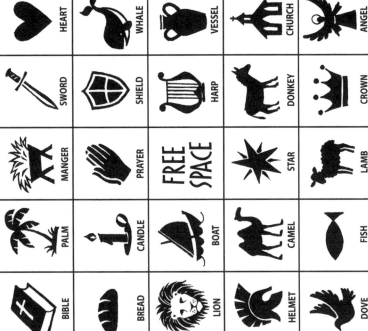

HEART	SWORD	MANGER	PALM	BIBLE
WHALE	SHIELD	PRAYER	CANDLE	BREAD
VESSEL	HARP	FREE SPACE	BOAT	LION
CHURCH	DONKEY	STAR	CAMEL	HELMET
ANGEL	CROWN	LAMB	FISH	DOVE

BIBLE STORY

BINGO

LAMB	FISH	DOVE	CHURCH	DONKEY
MANGER	PALM	BIBLE	ANGEL	CROWN
CANDLE	BREAD	FREE SPACE	HEART	SWORD
ARK	LION	WHALE	SHIELD	PRAYER
STAR	CAMEL	HELMET	VESSEL	HARP

Travel Scavenger Hunt

 AIRPLANE ☐

 BOAT ☐

 BRIDGE ☐

 CHURCH ☐

 TRACTOR ☐

 CAMPER ☐

 TRAFFIC LIGHT ☐

 BIKE ☐

 HORSE ☐

 FIRE HYDRANT ☐

 STOP SIGN ☐

 COW ☐

Around-The-House Scavenger Hunt

 CRAYON ☐

 YARN ☐

 SUNGLASSES ☐

 FEATHER ☐

 COMB ☐

 CANDY ☐

 KITCHEN SPOON ☐

 KEY ☐

 SOCK ☐

 PUZZLE PIECE ☐

 COIN ☐

 PAPER CLIP ☐

PHOTOCOPY THIS PAGE FOR MULTIPLE USES.

BIBLE STORY BINGO

Card 1:

B	I	N	G	O
CROWN	ANGEL	BIBLE	PALM	MANGER
SWORD	HEART	BREAD	CANDLE	PRAYER
SHIELD	WHALE	FREE SPACE	LION	BOAT
HARP	VESSEL	HELMET	CAMEL	STAR
DONKEY	CHURCH	DOVE	FISH	LAMB

BIBLE STORY BINGO

Card 2:

B	I	N	G	O
ANGEL	BIBLE	PALM	MANGER	SWORD
HEART	BREAD	CANDLE	PRAYER	SHIELD
WHALE	LION	FREE SPACE	ARK	HARP
VESSEL	HELMET	CAMEL	STAR	DONKEY
CHURCH	DOVE	FISH	LAMB	CROWN

Ladybug – Match Two

Only two of these ladybigs are exactly alike. Can you spot them?

Spotted Pony – Match the Spots

Look closely! There are eight sets of matching spots.
Draw a line to connect each matching set.

BIBLE STORY BINGO

FISH	LAMB	CROWN	ANGEL	BIBLE
PALM	MANGER	SWORD	HEART	BREAD
CANDLE	PRAYER	FREE SPACE	SHIELD	WHALE
LION	BOAT	HARP	VESSEL	HELMET
CAMEL	STAR	DONKEY	CHURCH	DOVE

BIBLE STORY BINGO

LAMB	CROWN	ANGEL	PALM	BIBLE
MANGER	SWORD	HEART	CANDLE	BREAD
PRAYER	SHIELD	FREE SPACE	LION	WHALE
ARK	HARP	VESSEL	CAMEL	HELMET
STAR	DONKEY	DOVE	FISH	CHURCH

Mountain Maze

Find the path to the top without crossing over any lines or rocks.

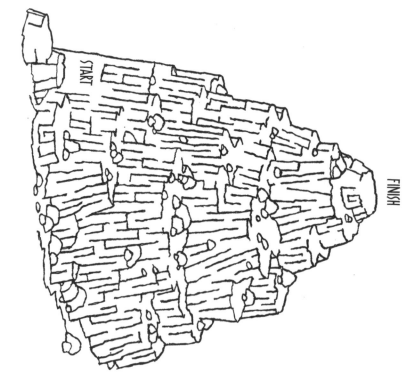

START

FINISH

Wild Journey Maze

Find your way through this untamed land to get to the river on the other side. Watch out for those snakes!

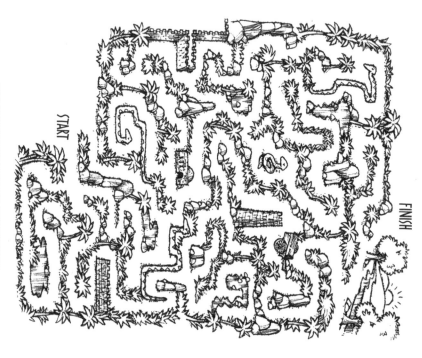

START

FINISH

BIBLE STORY BINGO

BIBLE STORY BINGO

BIBLE STORY

BINGO

B	I	N	G	O
BIBLE	CANDLE	BREAD	HEART	SWORD
PRAYER	VESSEL	HARP	BOAT	LION
HELMET	DOVE	CHURCH	BIBLE	DONKEY
FISH	WHALE	SHIELD	ARK	ANGEL
LION	DOVE	CHURCH	BOAT	DONKEY
FISH	CANDLE	BREAD	HEART	SWORD
PRAYER	ANGEL	CROWN	LAMB	HELMET
ARK				

N	G	O	B	I
MANGER	PALM			
WHALE	SHIELD			
STAR	CAMEL			
CROWN	LAMB			
STAR	CAMEL			
MANGER	PALM			
VESSEL	HARP			

| | | FREE SPACE | | |

Ancient City Maze

Enter the ancient city, tour around, and find your way out!

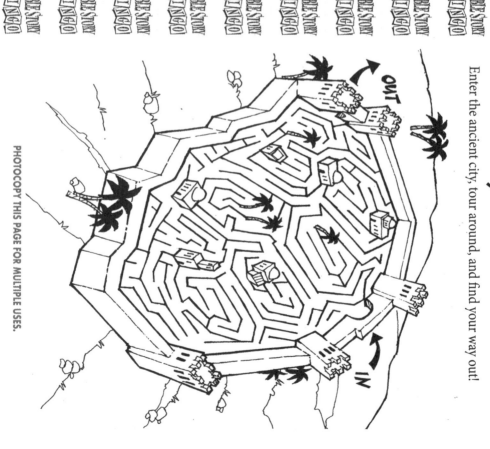